Bridges

KATIE MARSICO

Children's Press®
An Imprint of Scholastic Inc.

Content Consultant

Matthew Lammi, PhD

Assistant Professor

Department of Science, Technology,

Engineering, and Mathematics Education

North Carolina State University

Raleigh, North Carolina

Library of Congress Cataloging-in-Publication Data

Marsico, Katie, 1980– author.

Bridges / by Katie Marsico.

pages cm. — (A true book)

Summary: "Learn all about some of the world's most incredible bridges, from how they are designed and built to how bridge technology has changed over time."— Provided by publisher.

Includes bibliographical references and index.

ISBN 978-0-531-22479-3 (library binding) — ISBN 978-0-531-22269-0 (pbk.)

1. Bridges—Juvenile literature. 2. Bridges—Design and construction—Juvenile literature. I. Title. II. Series: True book.

TG148.M37 2016

624.2—dc23   2015023727

© 2016 Scholastic Inc.

All rights reserved. Published in 2016 by Children's Press, an imprint of Scholastic Inc.

Printed in China 62

SCHOLASTIC, CHILDREN'S PRESS, A TRUE BOOK™, and associated logos are trademarks and/or registered trademarks of Scholastic Inc.

1 2 3 4 5 6 7 8 9 10 R 25 24 23 22 21 20 19 18 17 16

Front cover: The Dragon King Bridge in Changsha, China
Back cover: Construction on the San Francisco-Oakland Bay Bridge

Find the Truth!

Everything you are about to read is true *except* for one of the sentences on this page.

Which one is **TRUE**?

T or F The Romans were famous for building arch bridges.

T or F An earthquake destroyed the Tacoma Narrows Bridge.

Find the answers in this book.

Contents

THE **BIG** TRUTH!

Brave the Bridge!

People cross the Brooklyn Bridge in New York CIty.

The first drawbridges were probably built in France.

CHAPTER 1

Incredible Connectors

Imagine traveling from Sausalito, California, on one side of the San Francisco Bay to San Francisco on the other. The trip itself is only about 10 miles (16 kilometers). However, it involves crossing extremely deep water swirling with strong currents. You could take a ferry or plane across. Yet the Golden Gate Bridge is easier! Driving, biking, or even walking over the bridge are all options.

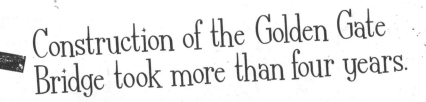

Construction of the Golden Gate Bridge took more than four years.

Connecting People

The Golden Gate Bridge spans 1.7 miles (2.7 km) from one **abutment** to the other. Between its May 1937 opening and January 2014, more than 2 billion vehicles traveled across it. Today, it serves as a major U.S. landmark. More importantly, the Golden Gate Bridge—like so many bridges—helps keep people connected. It supports travel and trade while linking communities that are separated by water.

Roughly 40 million cars cross the Golden Gate Bridge each year.

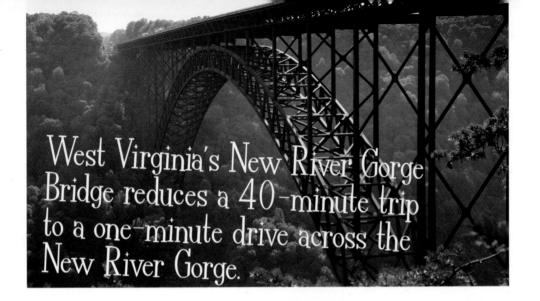

West Virginia's New River Gorge Bridge reduces a 40-minute trip to a one-minute drive across the New River Gorge.

Providing Passage

Bridges provide passage over an obstacle such as a body of water or a **depression**. Often, they stretch across train tracks and roads. Different bridges are meant to support different loads. Some are mainly used for foot traffic, or walking. Others are built to hold several thousand tons of weight on a daily basis. Bridges may be natural structures such as tangled tree roots or fallen logs. Others are made up of massive amounts of concrete and steel. Many of these bridges are engineering wonders.

A bridge must be carefully designed and constructed, and then maintained throughout its lifetime.

The Right Design

Designing and building safe, sturdy bridges is a challenging process. Engineers and architects must design structures that can withstand **corrosion**, powerful winds, and natural disasters such as earthquakes. This strength must be balanced against trade-offs such as cost. A community must be able to afford the work and materials that go into building a bridge.

For architects and engineers, building bridges involves overcoming unique obstacles. But bridge building also presents opportunities for creative thinking. People are forever finding ways to improve construction. They're also envisioning new designs and potential uses for bridges. As a result, the world will continue to rely on these engineering wonders for a long time to come.

Bridge designs will continue to change over time as designers innovate.

The Mackinac Bridge in Michigan is the longest **suspension** bridge in the Western Hemisphere.

Spanning the Centuries

The very first bridges ever used were natural, such as sand banks or rock arches. With time, humans figured out ways to construct their own bridges. At first, they used whatever materials were easily at hand. Over the centuries, humans learned how to manipulate and create new, sturdier materials. They also experimented with bridge designs that were more complicated and more challenging to construct.

Basic Beginnings

The earliest bridges made by humans were relatively simple. Most were basic beam bridges. They went straight across an obstacle, sometimes with vertical supports underneath. These first bridges were made from logs, stones, rocks, tree roots, sand, or dirt. These materials alone didn't always support stable or long-lasting construction. As a result, storms and rainwater often wore ancient bridges down as time passed. In addition, early bridges didn't usually span great distances.

The Tarr Steps make up a heavy stone bridge in Somerset, England, and date back several hundred years.

Sturdy building materials helped ensure Roman bridges lasted centuries.

Improvements in Ancient Rome

Several advances in bridge building occurred in the Roman Empire (27 BCE–476 CE). For a start, the ancient Romans used an early form of cement called pozzolana in their construction. Pozzolana was made from a mixture of water, lime, sand, and volcanic rock. Working with cement allowed the Romans to create sturdier, stronger bridges than before. Their structures could be larger and capable of supporting more weight.

The Romans also began constructing bridges with an arch, or curve. A support called an abutment was on either side of the bridge where the curve met the ground. This kept the arch stable. When people crossed, the pressure of their weight was distributed along the arch, into the abutment. This strong design made it possible to build lightweight bridges that supported heavier loads. The Romans built more than 1,000 arch bridges throughout their vast empire. The bridges helped the Romans travel efficiently and establish trade routes through Europe, Asia, and Africa.

Weight distributes along arch

Abutment

Some Roman bridges, such as this one in Spain, were designed with several arches.

Up or Down?

During the Middle Ages (500–1500 CE), bridges were frequently used for defense. People often constructed cities and castles within walls surrounded by water-filled ditches called moats. They lowered bridges known as drawbridges over the moats to let certain people in. They raised the drawbridges to keep enemies out. Drawbridges are still used today, often over waterways. The drawbridges are lowered and raised to accommodate boat traffic moving underneath.

Making steel was a hot and often dangerous job during the Industrial Revolution.

The Age of Iron and Steel

During the late 18th and early 19th centuries, the Industrial Revolution occurred in nations such as Great Britain and the United States. This period included many exciting advances in technology and launched an era of rapid industrial growth. It also led to the mass production of sturdier building materials such as cast iron.

In 1779, engineers and architects completed the first cast-iron bridge, near Coalbrookdale, England. Known as the Iron Bridge, this structure spanned the River Severn. It provided a safer, faster alternative to using a ferry to transport people and goods across the water. As the Industrial Revolution progressed, steel became another popular building material. Such **innovations**, or improvements, paved the way for architects and engineers to design larger, longer bridges that continue to connect communities around the world to this day.

The Iron Bridge still stands in England and is used regularly.

The Victoria Falls Bridge crosses the Zambezi River between Zimbabwe and Zambia, passing close to the massive Victoria Falls.

CHAPTER 3

Bridge Building

Today, bridges are built in a wide variety of shapes and sizes. Each bridge's particular design depends on many factors. A bridge's intended use, the length it must span, and the area's climate are a few examples. Most use a combination of building materials such as concrete and steel. Their structures typically fall into one of four main groups. These are beam bridges, arch bridges, **cantilever** bridges, and suspension bridges.

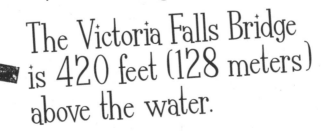

The Victoria Falls Bridge is 420 feet (128 meters) above the water.

Beam

Pillars

The Lake Pontchartrain Causeway is the world's longest continuous bridge over water.

Beams and Arches

Beam bridges consist of a horizontal beam supported on either end by piers, or pillars. Lake Pontchartrain Causeway in Louisiana and the Zoo Bridge in Cologne, Germany, are both beam bridges.

Just like ancient Roman bridges, arch bridges have a curved surface that rests on abutments. Well-known arch bridges include the New River Gorge Bridge in West Virginia and Australia's Sydney Harbour Bridge.

Cantilevers

A cantilever is a long beam that's fixed, or fastened in place, at only one end. Cantilever bridges generally feature pairs of back-to-back cantilevers with a beam bridge between them. The Commodore John Barry Bridge is a cantilever bridge. It stretches between Bridgeport, New Jersey, and Chester, Pennsylvania. The Minato Bridge between Osaka and Amagasaki, Japan, is also a cantilever bridge.

Span suspended between two cantilever arms

Cantilever

Cantilever

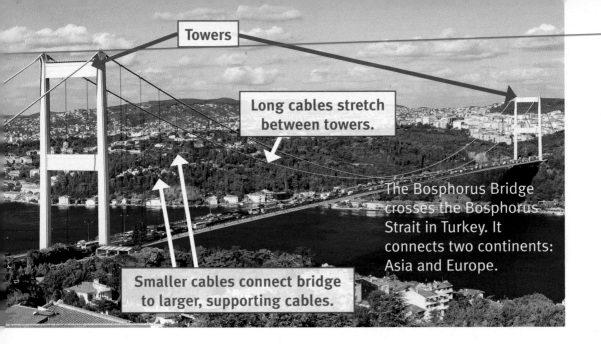

Towers

Long cables stretch between towers.

Smaller cables connect bridge to larger, supporting cables.

The Bosphorus Bridge crosses the Bosphorus Strait in Turkey. It connects two continents: Asia and Europe.

Suspension Bridges

Suspension bridges are supported by vertical cables. These cables are suspended, or hung, between larger cables that stretch between two or more towers. Famous examples of suspension bridges are the Golden Gate Bridge in San Francisco, California, and the George Washington Bridge in New York City. Others are the two bridges over the Bosphorus Strait in Istanbul, Turkey, and the Humber Bridge near Hull, England.

Withstanding Wind

Bridges must be able to withstand a variety of natural forces, including destructive windstorms. The need to make bridges more wind resistant became obvious on November 7, 1940. That day, powerful gusts triggered the collapse of the Tacoma Narrows Bridge over Puget Sound in Washington State. Though the bridge was destroyed, no human lives were lost.

A man runs off the Tacoma Narrows Bridge not long before it collapses.

The Tacoma Narrows Bridge disaster proved that strong winds can cause dangerous vibrations. This is true even when sturdy building materials such as steel are used. Architects and engineers responded by designing more **aerodynamic** bridges. To do this, designers first determine the typical direction of wind forces in a given area. Then they design the bridge so that solid building materials face away from oncoming gusts. Wind then moves around bridges without causing them to sway too much.

A Timeline of Bridge Innovations

27 BCE–476 CE

The Roman Empire uses concrete and arches to build sturdy, long-lasting bridges.

18th–19th centuries

Designers begin building bridges using cast iron and steel.

Easing the Impact of Earthquakes

Bridges also need to remain stable during earthquakes. Many architects and engineers achieve this by making bridges **flexible**. The structures can gently sway if the ground shakes. Piers and columns that can move slightly ease the overall impact of the motion triggered by an earthquake. Flexibility is an especially important feature in areas such as California, where earthquakes are more likely to occur.

2014

Workers add solar cells to Blackfriars Bridge, making it the largest bridge to produce solar power.

2008

The first bridge made with a new material called fiber-reinforced plastic opens to traffic in Maine.

Brave the Bridge!

Bridges help people get where they need to go. Sometimes, however, they make for an exciting—and potentially terrifying—adventure. Dizzying heights, narrow curves, and shaky footing all add to the thrill of crossing the structures described below.

Don't Look Down!

The Royal Gorge Bridge stretches 1,270 feet (387 m) across a gorge in Cañon City, Colorado. The view from this suspension bridge can be overwhelming for anyone afraid of heights. People crossing the bridge can spy the Arkansas River 956 feet (291 m) below. That's the same as peering down from atop an 88-story building!

Somewhat Shaky

The Capilano Suspension Bridge in North Vancouver, Canada, stretches 450 feet (137 m). It is situated 230 feet (70 m) above an evergreen forest. At this height, some travelers may wish that the bridge were a little less shaky. The bridge's cedar planks bounce on their steel cables when people cross!

Watch the Weather!

The William Preston Lane Jr. Memorial Bridge reaches across the Chesapeake Bay. Most of its rougly 5-mile (8 km) span is a suspension bridge. At its tallest point, the bridge rises 186 feet (57 m) above the water. Drivers who have been stuck in the middle of the bridge during intense storms report that they completely lose sight of land.

Tall and Tight

The suspended footbridges of the Kakum Canopy Walk in Ghana have railings and net sides. Travelers cling to them for roughly 1,000 feet (300 m). This intense journey takes place 100 feet (30 m) above the forest floor on a wooden plank that's just 1 foot (0.3 m) wide!

The World's Best-Known Bridges

Bridges aren't merely about building materials and structural patterns. These engineering wonders are also examples of extreme architecture. For instance, the Danyang–Kunshan Grand Bridge is currently the world's longest aggregate bridge. An aggregate bridge is made up of many connected small bridges. Located in China's Jiangsu Province, it spans more than 102 miles (164 km).

The Danyang-Kunshan Grand Bridge carries high-speed trains.

The Millau Viaduct crosses the valley surrounding the Tarn River in southern France.

Other Extremes

The world's tallest bridge is situated in Millau-Creissels, France. One of the **masts** on the Millau **Viaduct** reaches a height of 1,125 feet (343 m).

Not all record-breaking bridges are famous because of their size. The Caravan Bridge in Izmir, Turkey, is known for its age. It dates back to 850 BCE and is still crossed regularly. This makes it the world's oldest functioning bridge.

Legendary Landmarks

Many bridges also serve as geographical landmarks. People frequently link the image of the Golden Gate Bridge to San Francisco, California. They tend to establish a similar connection between the Brooklyn Bridge and New York City. The Tower Bridge in London, England, and the Sydney Harbour Bridge in Sydney, Australia, are other world-famous landmarks.

The Brooklyn Bridge has a separate walkway for people crossing on foot or bike.

Different Designs

The Chengyang Wind and Rain Bridge stands out because of its unique design. This covered bridge is located in Qingdao in northeastern China. It stretches about 210 feet (64 m) across the Linxi River. The bridge's span includes a series of porches and **pavilions** that offer travelers protection against rain and wind. Thanks to the shelter it provides, the Chengyang Wind and Rain Bridge is a popular gathering place.

The Chengyang Wind and Rain Bridge was built in 1916.

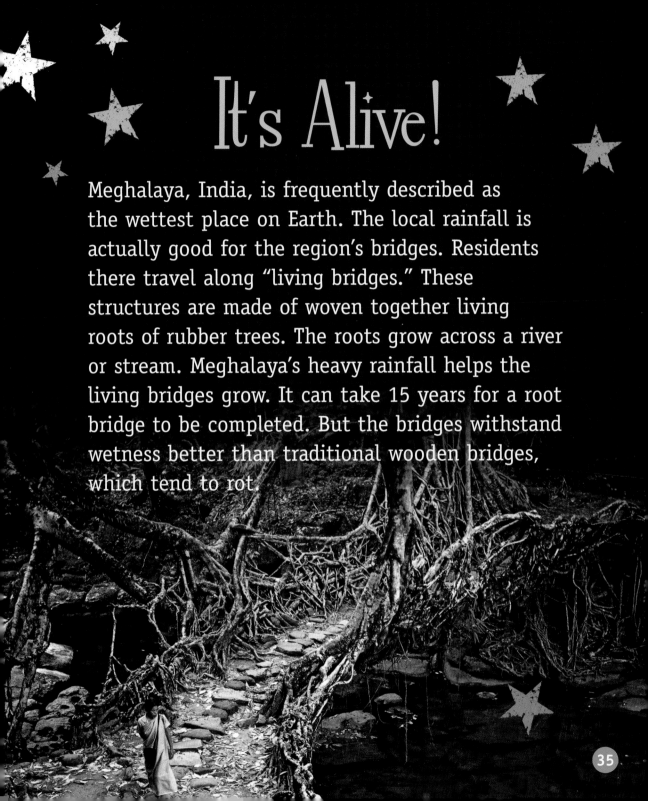

It's Alive!

Meghalaya, India, is frequently described as the wettest place on Earth. The local rainfall is actually good for the region's bridges. Residents there travel along "living bridges." These structures are made of woven together living roots of rubber trees. The roots grow across a river or stream. Meghalaya's heavy rainfall helps the living bridges grow. It can take 15 years for a root bridge to be completed. But the bridges withstand wetness better than traditional wooden bridges, which tend to rot.

Crossing Into the Future

It's impossible to predict all the remarkable innovations that will be used to build bridges in the years to come. What's certain is that people are determined to find new ways of making bridges both stronger and more environmentally friendly. In the process, designers are also constantly envisioning how to shape bridges into symbols of the modern world.

The Millennium Bridge in London was the first crossing built over the River Thames in 100 years.

Fiber-reinforced plastics and similar materials make up nearly half of a 787 airplane.

New Blends of Building Materials

Recently, architects and engineers have begun combining materials to both repair and construct bridges. **Hybrid** designs, which use a blend of different materials, often involve concrete, steel, and fiber-reinforced plastics (FRPs). FRPs consist of plastic wrapped around fibers, or thin threads, made from materials such as carbon and glass. They're used to produce a variety of items, including surfboards and aircraft wings.

FRPs are lightweight but strong and don't corrode as easily as metal and stone. For this reason, some designers have begun to incorporate them in bridges. The Neal Bridge in Pittsfield, Maine, was the first bridge in the world built with FRP arches. It opened to traffic in late 2008. Architects and engineers hope it will encourage the development of additional hybrid designs.

This close-up photo of fiberglass, a type of FRP, shows how its fibers are woven together.

Aiding the Environment

The bridges of the future also represent unique opportunities to support and protect the environment. For example, in early 2014, London, England, became home to the world's largest solar-powered bridge. Blackfriars Bridge spans the River Thames and is used for railway traffic. The bridge features a roof that has 4,400 solar panels. Each panel on Blackfriars Bridge converts sunlight into electric energy, which is used to power the Blackfriars railroad station.

Blackfriars Bridge has become a recognizable landmark in London.

It took years for workers to intall all 4,400 solar panels on Blackfriars Bridge.

By creating solar power, the bridge helps reduce pollution. When trains use coal, gasoline, or other carbon-based fuels to operate, the trains release various carbon gases into the air. These gases pollute the environment. When solar energy is a source of electricity—as it is for the electric trains that cross Blackfriars Bridge—carbon-based fuel is not needed. This results in less pollution.

Skyscraper bridges are a new design based on an old idea. Older bridges such as Ponte Vecchio (left) in Italy contain shops and apartments.

Other Unique Uses

In the future, it's possible that engineers and architects will create many more exciting uses for bridges. Some people have discussed building entire cities—complete with residences and shops—on bridges. Others propose constructing skyscraper bridges. These structures would connect different areas while also serving as buildings with office space and meeting halls.

The possibilities for future bridges appear endless. Bridge designers and builders have shown that they'll continue to move forward when it comes to design and construction. Undoubtedly, they'll build upon the innovative ideas that have been used to create bridges in the past. The result will be even more remarkable bridges, all helping connect the world. ★

A bridge completed in 2014 takes visitors between ruins of castles and forts in the Austrian Alps.

The span of the Golden Gate Bridge: 1.7 mi. (2.7 km)

Number of vehicles that crossed the Golden Gate Bridge between May 1937 and January 2014: More than 2 billion

Date the Tacoma Narrows Bridge collapsed: November 7, 1940

Width of the plank people travel along on the Kakum Canopy Walk: 1 ft. (0.3 m)

Length of the Danyang–Kunshan Grand Bridge (the world's longest bridge): More than 102 mi. (164 km)

Height of one of the masts on the Millau Viaduct (the world's tallest bridge): 1,125 ft. (343 m)

Number of solar panels on the roof of Blackfriars Bridge: 4,400

Did you find the truth?

T The Romans were famous for building arch bridges.

F An earthquake destroyed the Tacoma Narrows Bridge.

Resources

Books

Mattern, Joanne. *Bridges*. Vero Beach, FL: Rourke Educational Media, 2015.

Squire, Ann O. *Extreme Bridges*. New York: Children's Press, 2015.

Stine, Megan. *Where Is the Brooklyn Bridge?* New York: Grosset & Dunlap, 2016.

Visit this Scholastic Web site for more information on bridges:
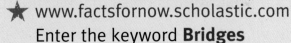 www.factsfornow.scholastic.com
Enter the keyword **Bridges**

Important Words

abutment (uh-BUT-muhnt) — a heavy structure that supports a bridge or other construction

aerodynamic (air-oh-dye-NAM-ik) — designed to move through the air very easily and quickly

cantilever (KAN-tuh-lee-vur) — a long piece of wood, metal, or other material that sticks out from a structure to act as a support

corrosion (kuh-ROH-zhuhn) — the process of being slowly broken down and destroyed

depression (di-PREH-shuhn) — a hollow or sunken place on Earth's surface

flexible (FLEK-suh-buhl) — able to bend

hybrid (HYE-brid) — something that is made by combining two or more things

innovations (in-uh-VAY-shunz) — new ideas or methods

masts (MASTS) — tall, vertical poles that rise up from bridges

pavilions (puh-VIL-yuhnz) — open buildings that are often used as shelter or recreation

suspension (suh-SPEN-shuhn) — the state of being attached to a support and hanging downward

viaduct (VYE-uh-duhkt) — a bridge that carries a railroad track, road, or pipeline across a valley or over a city street

Index

Page numbers in **bold** indicate illustrations.

About the Author

Katie Marsico graduated from Northwestern University and worked as an editor in reference publishing before she began writing in 2006. Since that time, she has published more than 200 titles for children and young adults. Ms. Marsico's favorite bridge in the world is the John Ringling Causeway in Sarasota County, Florida.